SNOW LEOPARDS

BY SOPHIE GEISTER-JONES

WWW.APEXEDITIONS.COM

Copyright © 2022 by Apex Editions, Mendota Heights, MN 55120. All rights reserved. No part of this book may be reproduced or utilized in any form or by any means without written permission from the publisher.

Apex is distributed by North Star Editions:
sales@northstareditions.com | 888-417-0195

Produced for Apex by Red Line Editorial.

Photographs ©: Shutterstock Images, cover, 1, 4–5, 6, 7, 8–9, 10–11, 12–13, 14–15, 16–17, 18–19, 20, 21, 22–23, 24–25, 26, 27, 29

Library of Congress Control Number: 2020952942

ISBN
978-1-63738-034-5 (hardcover)
978-1-63738-070-3 (paperback)
978-1-63738-138-0 (ebook pdf)
978-1-63738-106-9 (hosted ebook)

Printed in the United States of America
Mankato, MN
082021

NOTE TO PARENTS AND EDUCATORS

Apex books are designed to build literacy skills in striving readers. Exciting, high-interest content attracts and holds readers' attention. The text is carefully leveled to allow students to achieve success quickly. Additional features, such as bolded glossary words for difficult terms, help build comprehension.

TABLE OF CONTENTS

CHAPTER 1

GHOST OF THE MOUNTAIN

A snow leopard walks through the snowy trees. She moves without making a sound. Her pale fur makes her nearly invisible.

Snow leopards rarely live in groups, unless they are raising babies.

Two fluffy cubs run after her.

They jump and play in the snow.

Snow leopards are born in dens. Later, the mother teaches her babies to hunt.

A cub stays with its mother
for just under two years.

Snow leopards
usually have two to
three cubs at a time.

Suddenly, the mother tenses. She senses danger. She nudges her cubs to run. But one cub is too slow. So, she picks it up with her mouth. Then she runs away.

Snow leopards can run as fast as 40 miles per hour (64 km/h).

FOOTPRINTS IN THE SNOW

Snow leopards are hard to see in the wild. Scientists sometimes study their tracks. But even tracks are rare. As a result, people have much to learn about snow leopards.

CHAPTER 2

COLD-WEATHER CATS

Snow leopards live on tall mountains throughout Asia. These mountains are rocky and cold.

Many snow leopards live in Central Asia. Some live farther north or south.

Snow leopards thrive in this harsh **environment**. Their thick fur keeps them warm. Their noses help, too. They heat the air that the cats breathe.

Some snow leopards live in the Himalayas. These are the highest mountains on Earth.

A snow leopard's fluffy fur can be 2 to 4 inches (5–10 cm) long.

A snow leopard can travel 25 miles (40 km) in one day.

Most snow leopards live alone. They roam large **territories**. But their **habitat** is shrinking. As a result, the number of snow leopards is going down, too.

KEYSTONE SPECIES

Snow leopards are a **keystone species**. If they are doing well, it's a sign that the rest of their habitat is healthy. But if they struggle, so do many other animals and plants.

CHAPTER 3

FUR AND TAILS

A snow leopard's body is a great fit for its mountain home. Its fur is gray and white. It has black spots. The spots act as **camouflage**.

An adult snow leopard weighs 50 to 90 pounds (23–41 kg).

A snow leopard's paws are big and wide. They act like snowshoes. They spread out the cat's weight so it doesn't sink into the snow.

Snow leopards are good at running or jumping down steep slopes.

A snow leopard's back legs are longer than its front legs. This helps the cat climb.

Snow leopards have long, thick tails. They use their tails for balance.

Snow leopards can leap up to 50 feet (15 m).

A snow leopard's tail can be nearly as long as its body.

Snow leopards can sleep as much as 18 hours each day.

SOFT TAIL

A snow leopard wraps its tail around its body when it sleeps. The tail acts like a blanket. It keeps the snow leopard warm.

CHAPTER 4

ON THE HUNT

Snow leopards hunt at night. They quietly creep up on their **prey**. When they are close, they pounce. They jump and grab their prey.

Snow leopards may run or jump down from high places to catch prey.

Snow leopards hunt both large and small animals.

24

A snow leopard bites its prey's throat. The cat uses its front paws, too. It grabs the prey with its claws.

Snow leopards can go two weeks between meals.

Snow leopards often catch blue sheep, ibexes, and yaks. They also eat birds and small animals. Snow leopards sometimes attack **livestock**. As a result, some people hunt and kill the cats.

Wild blue sheep climb high in the Himalayas.

Wild snow leopards often live for 15 to 18 years.

HUNTED CATS

Hunting is a big **threat** to snow leopards. Some people kill snow leopards to protect their livestock. **Poachers** hunt them as well. They sell the cats' body parts and fur.

COMPREHENSION QUESTIONS

Write your answers on a separate piece of paper.

1. Write a sentence describing how snow leopards hunt their prey.

2. Would you like to visit the mountains where snow leopards live? Why or why not?

3. What body parts act like snowshoes for snow leopards?

   A. their wide paws
   B. their thick fur
   C. their long tails

4. How does a snow leopard's fur help it blend in with its mountain home?

   A. Its fur has very bright colors.
   B. Its spots look like green plants.
   C. Its colors match the rocks and ice.

5. What does **pounce** mean in this book?

*When they are close, they **pounce**. They jump and grab their prey.*

    A. to listen to loud music

    B. to look at something shiny

    C. to jump on something to catch it

6. What does **tenses** mean in this book?

*Suddenly, the mother **tenses**. She senses danger.*

    A. gets nervous or scared

    B. feels safe and happy

    C. smells good food

Answer key on page 32.

GLOSSARY

camouflage
Colors or markings that help animals blend in with the area around them.

environment
The surroundings of living things in a particular place.

habitat
The type of place where animals normally live.

keystone species
A plant or animal that is important for the health of all other living things in an area.

livestock
Animals kept and cared for by humans. Some examples are sheep, cows, and chickens.

poachers
People who hunt where or when hunting is against the law.

prey
An animal that is hunted and eaten by another animal.

territories
Areas that animals or groups of animals live in and defend.

threat
Something that is likely to cause danger or harm.

TO LEARN MORE

BOOKS

Hogan, Christa C. *Mountain Lions*. Lake Elmo, MN: Focus Readers, 2017.

Shaffer, Lindsay. *Snow Leopards*. Minneapolis: Bellwether Media, 2020.

Thomas, Rachael L. *Animal Camouflage Clash*. Minneapolis: Abdo Publishing, 2020.

ONLINE RESOURCES

Visit **www.apexeditions.com** to find links and resources related to this title.

ABOUT THE AUTHOR

Sophie Geister-Jones lives in Saint Paul, Minnesota. She loves reading. She and her brothers have a book club.

INDEX

Answer Key:
1. Answers will vary; 2. Answers will vary; 3. A; 4. C; 5. C; 6. A